HENDERSON'S
HOUSE RULES

"My hope for the world is that, through consideration and common sense, we can all get along. Barring that, there's *Henderson's House Rules*. It's equal parts referee, judge, and Emily Post. And if you disagree with a ruling, it might prompt you to come up with your own version."

—Doug Janz, sportswriter and journalist

"After years as a marriage counselor and seeing innumerable general-interest books on relationships, *Henderson's* is truly a breath of fresh air. It's a charming book. Yes, couples really do argue over the correct way to use a kitchen sponge. But perhaps now they can avoid such tedious arguments—and even end up laughing at themselves."

—Sally Maison, PhD, retired psychologist, Meta Resources, St. Paul, MN

HENDERSON'S HOUSE RULES

The Official Guide to Replacing the Toilet Paper and Other Domestic Topics of Great Dispute

by E.L. Henderson and David E. O'Connor

Illustrated by Steven Edwards

East Quincy Publishing

Johnson City, Tennessee

East Quincy Publishing
P.O. Box 851, Johnson City, Tennessee 37605
Visit us online at www.EastQuincyPublishing.com

First printing 2005

ISBN 0-9764078-0-9

LCCN 2004117127

Illustrated by Steven Edwards
Design by Freshpunch

Disclaimer
The authors have tried to provide quality information but make no guarantees
about its accuracy or completeness. Indeed, for some people or in some
situations, the information may be inappropriate, inaccurate or incorrect.

References to proprietary material are without the owners' permission
and do not constitute their endorsement of this book or our endorsement
of their material.

To Sharon

It is much more material that there should be a rule to go by than what the rule is.

—Thomas Jefferson
A Manual of Parliamentary Practice, 1801

Contents

Preamble   **1**
"We would never argue over such a petty issue"

§1: The Kitchen   **6**
1.1. Loading the dishwasher
1.2. Unloading the dishwasher
1.3. Soaking dirty dishes in the sink
1.4. Washing dishes by hand
1.5. Pet dishes and pets eating off people dishes
1.6. The glasses on the shelf
1.7. The silverware (flatware) in the drawer
1.8. Coffee grounds down the sink
1.9. Sponges
1.10. Preparing food on countertops
1.11. Cutting boards
1.12. The toaster and other small appliances on the counters
1.13. Storing food on the shelves
1.14. Eating without a plate
1.15. Eating standing up
1.16. Eating or drinking from a container and putting it back in
       the refrigerator
1.17. Standing in front of the refrigerator with the door open
1.18. The milk and juice containers
1.19. Resealing bread and other items
1.20. Using the last of something: The "last useful amount"
1.21. Cooking
1.22. Cooking versus cleaning
1.23. Postponing cleaning after cooking
1.24. Cleaning up by guests

1.25. Cleaning rules for the kitchen
1.26. Trash and recyclables
1.27. Taking out the trash

§2: The Bedroom   38
2.1. Double beds
2.2. Pillows and bolsters on the floor
2.3. Making the bed
2.4. Décor
2.5. Things you can and can't do in bed if you don't sleep alone
2.6. Sex
2.7. Bedroom temperature
2.8. Clothes
2.9. Alarm clock
2.10. Pets in bedrooms
2.11. Shoes on the bed
2.12. Shoeless bedrooms
2.13. Towels from the bathroom
2.14. Trash
2.15. The top of the dresser

§3: The Laundry   50
3.1. Clean laundry
3.2. Dirty laundry
3.3. Doing another party's laundry
3.4. Laundry left where others can see it
3.5. Laundry left in machines
3.6. Laundry detergent

§4: The Bathroom   58

4.1. The door
4.2. Time spent in the bathroom
4.3. The toilet seat and lid
4.4. The toilet environs
4.5. The toilet paper
4.6. Flushing the toilet
4.7. Pets drinking out of the toilet
4.8. Cleaning the toilet after a single use
4.9. The toilet tank as storage area
4.10. Female "sanitary products"
4.11. The wastebasket
4.12. Teeth brushing and flossing
4.13. The soap in the shower
4.14. Wiping down the shower/bathtub
4.15. The tub and shower in general
4.16. Using another party's toiletries
4.17. Towels
4.18. The bathroom sink and cabinet

§5: The Rest of the House   78

5.1. Neatness level in general
5.2. The coffee table
5.3. Eating in the living room
5.4. Things you can't do in the living room
5.5. Storing mail
5.6. The phone
5.7. Music
5.8. Television
5.9. Reading the newspaper

5.10. Leaving lights on

5.11. Windows and shades

5.12. Décor

5.13. Cleaning other people's knickknacks, antiques, etc.

5.14. Clothes on furniture

5.15. The shoeless house

5.16. Houseguests

§6: The Exterior   **94**

6.1. The shared hallway

6.2. The porch

6.3. Smoking outdoors

6.4. The shared automobile

6.5. Parking

6.6. Shutting down the automobile

6.7. The handbrake

6.8. Maintaining the automobile interior

6.9. Gasoline

Acknowledgement   **103**

Index   **105**

Preamble

"We would never argue over such a petty issue."

Should the toilet paper be replaced so that it hangs over and out, away from the wall, or over and in, against the wall?

When you're done reading a section of the newspaper that your spouse or housemate hasn't read yet, should you fold it back to its original order or can you just leave it open?

Do the glasses go on the shelf rim-up or rim-down?

Does anyone really care?

Would anyone really argue over such minor things? Most people who live together or share living space together know that compromise is essential. But no one likes to be the person who makes the majority of the compromises. Every now and then the over-compromising person decides to stand firm on some seemingly petty issue—more on general principles than on strength of feelings about the particular issue at hand. Sometimes a person just has to say, "No, this time I'm not doing it your way." Meanwhile, the other person, who also feels that he or she is the one who makes most of the compromises, is astounded and offended that anyone would make such a fuss over something so trivial.

Why Domestic Harmony Is Like a Game of Cards

This book solves the problem of whose way is the right way so you don't have to compromise. It does the compromising for you—with definitive, authoritative answers to the many differing ways of doing everyday tasks. And from where does this authority come? What difference does it make? Who told Hoyle[1] he could decide the rules of card games? Who told Robert[2] he could dictate parliamentary rules of order? What matters is that there is a uniform set of rules. If playing a game of cards, for example, and a disagreement arises, do you attempt to compromise? To better communicate? No, you look up the rule, which settles the debate. This book serves a similar function.

And, as in card games and life, if the parties agree to a rule other than that set forth in this book, then they can and should follow that agreed-upon rule. If, for example, there is agreement that the toilet seat should always be left up, it should be left up—regardless of what this book says.

But authoritative is not the same as arbitrary. Hoyle and Robert wrote their rules on the basis of how most people did things and how well those ways worked. The same is done here. Sometimes the rationale behind a rule is given. It's easier to follow a rule that has a rationale behind it, even if you disagree with the rationale.

---

[1] Edmond Hoyle (1672–1769), English. He wrote the first rule books on whist and other games (but not poker).

[2] Henry Robert (1837–1923), American. He was an army officer who published a manual on parliamentary procedure in 1876: *Robert's Rules of Order*. Still in publication, it is often used by clubs and organizations desiring formal, orderly meetings.

Ways to Use This Book

You can use this book as a reference as disagreements arise. Check the rule and follow it. Inevitably, one party will think the rule is wrong—if both agreed on the rule, neither would be looking it up. But the rules are not biased in favor of one party. Sometimes a rule will favor the other party and you will just have to grin and bear it and go along, even if you know in your heart that the rule is wrong. The next time it will probably favor you, wrong though the other party may think the rule is.

Alternatively, you and the other members of the household (decision-making members, that is, not young children or guests) can sit down together and go through the book and use it as an outline to create your own rules. If there are two of you (husband and wife, for example) and you both agree on a rule, check it off and follow it. If you both agree a rule is wrong, correct it and follow what you both agree is the right way of doing things. This book sets forth rules, but its goal is harmony.

The authors apologize for the legalistic style of the book (though what did you expect from a book of rules?), especially the use of the word "party" as reference to a person. But the rules are House Rules, not just rules for married couples, and the word "party" is an easy way to refer to household members of all kinds, whether spouses, cohabiting couples, roommates, family members, or long-term guests.

Don't Take It Personally

It's not always as easy as it should be to follow a simple rule. By the time a person is old enough to live with someone else on a long-term basis, say twenty-five years old, just to pick an age, that person will have brushed his or her teeth (we hope) more than 18,000 times. If all those times a person was in the habit of leaving the cap off the toothpaste and is now expected to replace the cap, it would be foolish to expect 100 percent compliance. It would be even more foolish to take non-compliance personally. As previously stated, most of these so-called rules are minor, petty things. The goal is to decide on a way of doing them without feeling that you're the one who always gives in, and then to get on with the more important things in life!

§1

The Kitchen

1.1. Loading the dishwasher

For day-to-day use, the dishes don't have to be loaded in an orderly fashion. Only two things matter: (1) that the dirty dishes get put in the dishwasher, not left on the counter or in the sink; and (2) that they get loaded in a way that doesn't risk breakage. If you've had a big dinner and all the dishes aren't going to fit unless arranged in an orderly manner, then the rule is to arrange them in an orderly manner.

Silverware (flatware) can go in the silverware rack pointing up or down or both, unless the handles are small and will slip through the holes of the rack. Sharp knives and the like should point down. Very sharp small objects, such as the blades of a blender, are best put in a place more easily accessible (and noticeable) than the silverware holder, such as the top rack.

It should be obvious that dishes must be scraped before loading, but it is not necessary to rinse the dishes, glasses, cups, etc. before loading them. It's true that if a person puts an un-rinsed coffee cup in the upper tray, ugly coffee dregs will drip over the dirty dishes below. But so what? They're all going to be washed anyway. If, however, you have an old dishwasher that is marginally functional and won't clean dishes unless they are pre-washed, then you'll have to pre-wash them.

Some would argue that if you let dirty dishes sit too long in the dishwasher, food will become dried and caked on and not come off in the wash, especially if there is a preference for using the short or quick-wash cycle. It's a reasonable argument, but too much pre-cleaning defeats the work-saving benefits of having a dishwasher. Over 99 percent of the world lives without a dishwasher, so if you have one and use it, use it to its full advantage.

1.2. Unloading the dishwasher

In a magical world everyone would have two dishwashers, and you could take clean dishes out of one as needed and put dirty dishes in the other. But the world doesn't have room for so many billions of dishwashers, and for the rest of us with only one dishwasher, there are two schools of thought: (1) take out the clean dishes as you need them until the dishwasher is empty, then load it all at once with the accumulated dirty dishes; or (2) unload the clean dishes all at once and load the dirty dishes as they become dirty.

The House Rule is to unload the clean dishes all at once and load the dirty dishes as they become dirty.

But what do you do when the dishwasher is full of clean dishes and you've just had a glass of water? Are you suddenly obligated to unload the entire dishwasher just because you happened to be the first person to dirty a dish? See the following entry on soaking dishes in the sink and apply the spirit of the rule.

1.3. Soaking dirty dishes in the sink

You've downed a quick bowl of breakfast cereal and are about to dash off to your job at the World Bank. Should economic globalization wait while you unload the clean dishes from the dishwasher

Figure 1.2.

and load your dirty cereal bowl? No, you can give the bowl a quick rinse and leave it in the sink.

There are two reasons for leaving dishes unwashed in the sink. One is if they actually need to be soaked a bit before washing. However, a dish should soak no longer than is necessary to soften the food that has hardened on it. A half hour is more than enough time. After that, it becomes just another dirty dish in the sink. The other reason is if it's impractical—the dishwasher is full, you're rushing out the door late for work, or some other excuse of marginal acceptability.

This is the House Rule: Three items or 30 minutes. Once three items have accumulated in the sink, it's time to wash them, either by hand or by unloading the dishwasher and loading in the three dirty dishes. If anything has been in the sink for more than 30 minutes, it's time to wash it.

Regarding the argument that it's a more efficient use of time to let the dirty dishes build up and then deal with them all at once: Spending a minute to wash or load a dish or two generally uses dead time, whereas saving them up creates a time-consuming project. By taking care of a few dishes here and there, you lose nothing in time and gain much in neatness.

1.4. Washing dishes by hand

The correct way to wash dishes, in a perfect world, is to wash them in a sink or dishpan with warm soapy water, load them into the drain and rinse them with hot water all at once. Not many sinks are set up to do this. And if you're only washing a few items, this method isn't practical.

Thus, the House Rule: The person washing the

dishes gets to wash them as he or she prefers, even if using the soapy-sponge, one-dish-at-a-time method. Note that the rule assumes that the dishes are going to get clean (including the underside of each dish, the prongs of the forks, the handles of the knives) and that leaving the hot water running will be kept at a minimum. The concern over leaving the hot water running may require using a less wasteful method if there are a lot of dishes.

1.5. Pet dishes and pets eating off people dishes

Pet dishes may be washed with other dishes only if they are washed in a dishwasher. Otherwise, separately and with a different sponge. Pets may be allowed to eat off people dishes, unless one party objects. (Note that this is a House Rule; if pet training rules provide otherwise, that rule controls.)

1.6. The glasses on the shelf

Glasses go rim-up. An exception is when the shelves have no doors. Then the glasses can go rim-down—but be sure to keep the shelves clean. In all cases, expensive crystal should only go rim-up. If there are established rules for the care of expensive crystal, china, silverware, etc., those rules supersede these House Rules.

1.7. The silverware (flatware) in the drawer

Each piece (fork, knife, etc.) gets its own slot and should fit together, as the expression has it, like spoons in a drawer. Forks and spoons go in face-up. Knives go in pointed away from you, but do not need to have the sharp edge all facing the same way.

1.8. Coffee grounds down the sink

It is acceptable to put coffee grounds—from a French press coffee maker, for example—down the sink. The idea that coffee grounds will clog the sink is a popular, nearly universal misconception held even by people happy to use an in-sink garbage disposal, which grinds the garbage into particles much larger than coffee grounds.[3]

---

[3] Because coffee grounds move through the sink trap slowly, one is apt to find grounds in the trap when the blockage is actually caused by something else. This is correlation, not causation. However, our legal counsel, whose hourly rate is even greater than that of a plumber, insists that we remind the reader to follow this rule at one's own risk.

1.9. Sponges

There are several issues with sponges. The most important thing to keep in mind is that cellulose sponges are very cheap, and you can throw them away frequently. The idea of getting a lot of use from a sponge comes from the days of real sea sponges. They were expensive. The best kind of sea sponge, called a wool sponge, is still available though more expensive than ever. Wool sponges last for years, hold much more water, are gentle on the skin, and are interesting to look at. They make great bath sponges, but the cheap cellulose sponge is far better for kitchen use.

Never use the kitchen sponge to wipe things up off the floor. Keep a sponge under the sink or some other designated place for that. You may

use the same sponge for washing dishes that you use for wiping counters (see House Rule 1.10, "Preparing food on countertops").

As to leaving the sponge sopping wet in the sink as opposed to squeezed-out and placed on the edge of the sink: Contrary to that secret grudge one may be harboring, the other party doesn't drop the wet sponge in the sink out of neglect. It's most likely done out of the belief that it keeps the sponge moist and ready for use, whereas a squeezed-out sponge left on the edge of the sink soon becomes hard and dry and can't be used for a quick wipe until it's re-hydrated. So there is no House Rule. Both ways are acceptable, and there is no need for compromise: have two sponges, one hard and dry and useless on the edge of the sink, the other lying cold and wet and moldering at the bottom of the sink. In either case, be sure the sponges are not contaminated.

1.10. Preparing food on countertops

It is acceptable to prepare food (a sandwich, for example) directly on the kitchen counter rather than on a cutting board *only* if your kitchen

Figure 1.10.

counters are reserved for food preparation; that is, you keep them clean, you don't set grocery bags on the counters after those bags have been sitting in the bed of your pick-up truck or on the floor of a city bus, you don't have flies or other bugs, and your pets don't walk on the kitchen counters even when you're not around. Otherwise, food should be prepared on a cutting board.

1.11. Cutting boards

A cutting board is always required for cutting or chopping. Many kitchens have a separate cutting board for preparing raw meat. If so, segregation of use must be strictly followed. The two boards must, of course, be clearly distinguishable. Whether to use wood or plastic is a health issue, not a House Rule.[4]

1.12. The toaster and other small appliances on the counter

Some people believe that small appliances should be taken off the counter after each use and put away, even if the appliance is used every

---

[4] There currently seem to be two contrasting views: wood is better because bacteria die more quickly on wood boards; plastic is better because a plastic board can be put in the dishwasher.

day. This does make for neat counters and a tidy-looking kitchen. But the House Rule is otherwise. Items that are used daily or almost daily may be left on the counter. A toaster is a common example for many homes. Items that are used less often, a blender for example, should be put away. Because the number of appliances, frequency of use, and amount of counter space varies so much from home to home, it is recommended that the parties establish, in advance, a subset of rules on this issue.

Small appliances that are left out do not need to be unplugged unless the cord is in the way. The concept that toasters should be unplugged when not in use stems from the days before the pop-up toaster was invented. That was long ago. However, if your grandparents are visiting and it makes them nervous when the toaster is left plugged in, would it hurt so much to humor them? If you unplug the toaster, drape the plug-end of the cord over the toaster so that the person who goes to use it next will see that it needs to be plugged in and won't be wondering why the toast is taking so long while the eggs are getting cold.

1.13. Storing food on the shelves

Similar items should be grouped together; for example, all the soup cans should be kept in the same area. The cans and boxes do *not* have to be carefully aligned with the labels facing out. That's the House Rule. On the other hand, some people find great comfort in orderly shelves and experience a sense of unease when shelves are less orderly. It's a lot easier to make the effort to accommodate this mild compulsion than it is for the other party to overcome it. Likewise, it is easier for the "excessively orderly" person to rearrange things correctly on those occasions when the "disorderly" person puts something away wrong. Remember that the goal is harmony, not the rigid application of the rules.

1.14. Eating without a plate

This is also known as "sink eating" where, for example, a person eats a piece of cake over the sink so that the crumbs fall in the sink.

The House Rule is clear: All food must be put on a plate or on a napkin.

1.15. Eating standing up

Unless you're at an event such as a cocktail party, sit down to eat. Refueling in flight is rarely necessary. And if someone else prepared the food that you are treating as mere fuel, it's insulting.

1.16. Eating or drinking from a container and putting it back in the refrigerator

Never. Even if you're the only person in the household who eats or drinks that particular food or beverage. The scope of this House Rule extends to the issue of using clean utensils to eat out of containers. Thus it prohibits, for example, taking a clean spoon and scooping out one spoonful of ice cream.

(Note that this particular action would also violate House Rule 1.15, "Eating standing up.") The exception is a special container, such as a reusable water bottle, clearly labeled with one's name.

1.17. Standing in front of the refrigerator with the door open

Standing in front of the refrigerator with the door open is allowed. It is also permissible to leave the door open while you're carrying something to the table and you're coming back for another item. Although allowed, it is not a good practice—and the warmer the room, the more it's not a good idea.

But leaving the refrigerator door open is not the great sin some people feel it is. It was a serious offense in earlier times when refrigerators were not self-defrosting and the freezer unit was within the main section of the refrigerator. And when refrigerators were iceboxes, you opened them only for as long as necessary. If it drives you crazy to see people leave the refrigerator door open while they gaze into it wondering what they might like to eat, perhaps you are being influenced by these earlier times or, more likely, you internalized the rule from your parents, who picked it up from their parents.

Figure 1.17.

1.18. The milk and juice containers

It is not necessary to close the flap of cardboard cartons or put the cap back on a plastic jug after every use if the container is sitting on the table and you know that you or someone else will be taking more soon, unless you have flies or other bugs. Containers must be closed before returning them to the refrigerator. And they must be closed properly, particularly if the next person to use the item might give it a shake first, such as one might do with juice.

1.19. Resealing bread and other items

Bread generally comes sealed with a "twisty" or with a plastic tab. It is not necessary to replace the sealer after using the bread. Twisting the wrapper several times and folding it under the loaf itself will keep out air as just well as a twisty, and better than the plastic tab. Note that this rule applies only to food that can be sealed in this way. It's not an excuse for leaving a box of crackers open.

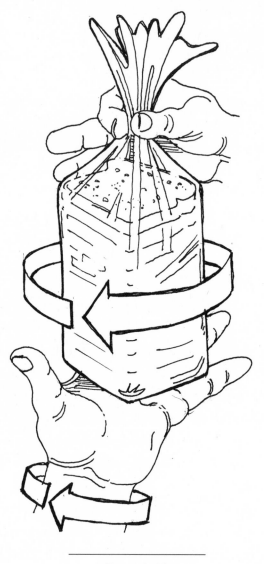

Figure 1.19.

1.20. Using the last of something: The "last useful amount"

When you use the last of something, the milk for example, the House Rule is that you write the item down on a shopping list and dispose of the empty container. If you eat the last of the leftover spaghetti, you are responsible for dealing with the dirty leftover container. This rule gives rise to the temptation never to use the last of anything and results in such behavior as returning a milk carton with a half-ounce of milk to the refrigerator.

"The last of something" therefore means the last *useful* amount. Such an amount will depend on numerous factors. If members of the household drink coffee and there is enough milk left to lighten one cup of coffee, that amount of milk should be saved. If there is enough cereal left for one-quarter of a serving, it should be thrown away (unless throwing away such an amount of food is objectionable on economic or moral grounds). Note that if you're returning the "last useful amount" of something to the refrigerator or cupboard, it is still your responsibility to add the item to the shopping list.

1.21. Cooking

There can be only one cook at a time. The other person is the helper. For purposes of these rules, the cook is referred to as the "chef," and anyone helping the cook is referred to as the "sous chef." ("Sous," pronounced like the name Sue, is French for "under," and it sounds much better than "helper.") In many families, one person is

always the chef, even if on occasion the sous chef does most of the work. In other situations, people take turns cooking. The rule is that the chef of the moment is the chef. Anyone else in the kitchen, regardless of his or her cooking skills, is, at best, a sous chef.

To illustrate: If Joe is cooking dinner, Joe is the chef. This remains true even if Joe is a terrible cook and his partner Jane, who usually cooks and who holds a degree from Le Cordon Bleu, is letting Joe cook his boiled Spam luncheon meat special for the evening.[5] Joe is the chef; Jane is the sous chef.

To further illustrate: If Jane is cooking and Joe's mother is visiting, Jane is the chef; Joe's mother is the sous chef. This remains true even if Jane's degree from Le Cordon Blue is a forgery and she can't boil water without burning the pan. Jane is the chef; Joe's mother is the sous chef. The sous chef never takes over any of the chef's duties without being directed to do so. The most common and most egregious example of not following this rule is when the sous chef decides to adjust the heat on the stove. Another example is "needs salt." A sous chef does not say "needs salt" to a chef. This is in contrast to the situation in which the chef directs the sous chef to check the heat on something or asks if the sous chef thinks something needs more salt.

---

[5] It is doubtful that anyone boils luncheon meat. For real recipes that actually sound good, the makers of Spam have a website with winning recipes from their annual national competition (www.spam.com, of course).

The House Rule that the chef is in charge also means that the chef gets to make up temporary rules for the kitchen. If the chef is boiling water in a pan without a cover, and the sous chef (or anyone else who happens to wander into the kitchen) believes he or she has solid scientific evidence that the water will come to a boil more quickly if the pan has a cover, the rule still applies: The chef is in charge, and if the chef wants a cover on the pan, the chef will put a cover on the pan or will direct the sous chef to do so. Alternatively, if the chef directs the officious intermeddler to get out of the kitchen, the officious intermeddler must get out of the kitchen.

1.22. Cooking versus cleaning

It is a widely held misconception that if one person cooks, the other person is obligated to clean up. This is not the House Rule. Cooking styles differ. Some cooks have the admirable ability to clean as they go. Others put all their focus into food preparation and leave cleaning until later. Because both styles are legitimate, the purported rule that the person who cooks

shouldn't have to clean doesn't work. There is no
House Rule on who cleans up after the cook. This
is a division-of-labor issue, not a House Rules
issue. We do, however, offer some guidelines.

When a cook is clean-as-you-go, it works well
for the non-cook to clean up after preparation.
If the cook is all-focus-on-cooking, it works well
for both to clean up after preparation.

1.23. Postponing cleaning after cooking

Postponing cleaning after cooking is generally a
bad idea. The food hardens. The joy of the meal
fades in memory in light of the immediate task
of cleaning plates, pots and pans crusted with
old food.

But there are times when it is most desirable to postpone cleaning after cooking. These are often happy occasions. Here are a few examples (and we hope there are many more)—a very early morning breakfast before heading out for a fishing trip; having friends over for a big meal in the evening; a quiet romantic meal for two followed by even more romantic events. Would you have it that after a wonderful meal, social intercourse is put on hold until the kitchen is cleaned? One would hope not. The House Rule: Clean as soon as possible after cooking unless there is a valid reason not to.

1.24. Cleaning up by guests

You have some friends over for dinner. They offer to help clean up, or perhaps they just start cleaning up. It is very temping to accept the help. The House Rule is otherwise. Guests can offer minor assistance, such as bringing their plate to the kitchen counter, but little more. That's the rule. If you would like a rationale, there are several. Some guests volunteer only out of a sense of duty. The guests don't know your kitchen and will work inefficiently, perhaps even inadvertently and destructively, using a Brillo pad on your best wine glasses, for example.

Let the guests relax and be guests. They aren't being lazy. You'll clean without their help and, presumably, at some point in the future they will reciprocate a dinner gathering, at which they will clean without your help. It all evens out. For those guests who insist on helping, reminding them of this fact is useful and allows them to refrain from helping without feeling guilty.

This rule does not apply to houseguests; that is, people staying at your house for a week or more. Houseguests are addressed briefly in §5: The Rest of the House.

1.25. Cleaning rules for the kitchen

Cleaning rules require a book of their own.[6] But some basic rules should be established among members of the household so as to avoid inadvertent damage. Examples of cleaning rules (the validity of which we do not address) are as follows: Do not use steel wool (e.g., Brillo

---

[6] And many exist. We would like to mention some here but do not wish to appear as endorsing any particular book.

or SOS pads) on stainless steel sinks because fibers from the steel wool become embedded in the metal of the sink and rust, causing a slight discoloration over time; do not use dish detergent on seasoned cast iron pans; do not use undiluted laundry bleach on porcelain sinks because it will harm the glaze. Thus, if a household member has a cleaning technique that he or she suspects may not be universal, that person should convey it to the other members of the household.

1.26. Trash and recyclables

Flatten such things as cereal boxes (open the bottom flaps and the box will fold up quite flat) and cardboard milk cartons before putting them in the trash or recycle bin. It is not generally necessary to open both ends of a can and flatten it unless you have a serious space problem. Why cartons and not cans? It takes very little effort to flatten cartons and it reduces space enormously. Cans take much more work. Items to be recycled should generally be given a quick rinse to remove food. If your community has a recycling program, it no doubt has its own rules.

If one person is always responsible for taking out the trash, he or she is exempt from the rule requiring flattening things.

1.27. Taking out the trash

Who takes out the trash is generally a division-of-labor issue, not a House Rules issue, but *when* to take it out is.[7] As used here, "to take out" means (assuming you're using plastic trashcan liners) taking out the full liner, sealing it, and replacing it with a new one.

The House Rule is, take out the trash (a) when the trash reaches the top[8] of the container, or (b) when there is anything in the trash that smells or will start to smell if left any longer. The trash container must be kept clean. Even when plastic liners are used, the trash container eventually becomes dirty. As to physically removing the full garbage bag from the house

---

[7] Do not apply the rule used by the popular television show *The Simpsons*: The person who adds the last piece of trash to the towering mound, causing an overflow onto the floor, has to take out the trash. (Bart: "Who tops it off, drops it off." Homer: "Nuh-uh, it isn't filled 'til it's spilled." Originally aired April 26, 1998.)

[8] Who is to say what is the top? Homer's rule would seem easier to follow: it either spills or it doesn't. But it didn't work for the Simpson household.

or apartment, there is no House Rule, but there are guidelines: It should be done as soon as is practical, which is usually immediately. But it does not need to be taken out immediately if that means going down into a dangerous alley late at night, nor does it need to be taken out immediately if the person responsible is planning to leave the house or apartment soon anyway and can take the trash on his or her way.

Figure 1.27.

§2

The Bedroom

2.1. Double beds

Who sleeps on which side of a double bed? The
woman gets to choose. The rationale: As a gross
generalization about culture-based gender issues
and some women's feelings of vulnerability,
many women tend not to sleep as well if their
side of the bed is near a window. For others, it's
when near a door.[9] Further, women are slightly
more likely than men to get up in the middle
of the night to use the bathroom and thus may
want to be closer to it.

2.2. Pillows and bolsters on the floor

Some people sit up in bed with extra pillows and
the like, then push them onto the floor when
turning out the light, the alternative being to get
out of a snug bed just as one is falling asleep and
transporting the pillows to their proper holding
area. The House Rule: No pillows on the floor.
The exception: if the bedroom is a shoeless room
and the floors kept quite clean.

---

[9] This assumes, of course, a man and a woman sleeping in the same bed,
but does not preclude other arrangements.

2.3. Making the bed

Sheets: The top sheet goes on the bed upside down so that when the top is folded over, the seam or pattern is facing right-side up and out.

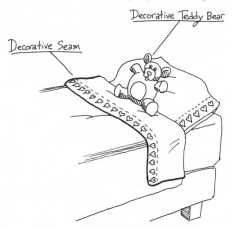

Decorative Teddy Bear

Decorative Seam

Each side of the bed is tucked in or not tucked in as decided by the person on that side. If one party wants the bottom tucked in and the other doesn't, it's possible to tuck in one half of the bottom and not the other. The answer to the mystery of why women tend to prefer the sheets tucked in tightly and men do not is that men are usually taller and their feet bigger, their legs extend down to the end of the bed, and if the sheets and blankets are tightly tucked in it can be uncomfortable.

The bed has to be made up every morning. However, it doesn't have to be made up perfectly as though company is coming (unless company is coming). In summer months, in warm climates, or if a partner suffers from night sweats, an excellent argument can be made for leaving the bed unmade during the day to let it air out—unmade but with the covers folded back neatly. But if either party objects, the House Rule prevails and the bed has to be made up every morning.

Although making the bed is important, simplicity is the goal if you don't sleep alone. Military (or hospital) corners are not required. They are also not prohibited: if one party wants to make the bed with military/hospital corners, that party is free to do so—but should not be offended when the other party undoes the corners when getting into bed.

Decorative pillows should be kept to a minimum. A party advocating more than three decorative pillows is responsible for their removal and storage when the bed is in use.

41

2.4. Décor

The issue with décor is when the parties share a bedroom and one party wants a particularly distinctive style—pink and frilly, for example, or guns and mounted moose heads on the walls. Bedrooms, for some reason, seem to attract extremes in décor.

The House Rule: No extremes.

2.5. Things you can and can't do in bed if you don't sleep alone

You can't floss your teeth or clip your nails. Other personal hygiene practices should not be engaged in without prior consent of one's bed partner. (The authors are aware that many activities—brushing a spouse's hair is but one of many examples—are quite appropriate for the bed and we hope that such things, when mutually agreed to, are continued.) You can't do any work you brought home from the office. You can't pay bills. But you can eat, if your partner doesn't object. You can watch television, read, or use your laptop computer if your partner doesn't object, but for only ten minutes after your partner wants to go to sleep.

2.6. Sex

You didn't really think there would be a House Rule on sex, did you?

2.7. Bedroom temperature

Some people like to sleep with the windows open in the middle of winter. Others like to sleep in a warm and toasty room. The rule is, no extremes. No colder than 60° F (16° C), no hotter than 75° F (25° C). The rule applies regardless of the source of heat or cold (e.g., an open window in winter, an air conditioner in summer). But a good night's sleep is an important thing, so if room temperature is more important to one party than the other, concede on the side of a lower temperature—one party can always add more blankets to his or her side or sleep in warmer bedclothes.

2.8. Clothes

Never on the floor. Draping clothes over a chair overnight is allowed. Note that this is only for overnight and for clothes that will either be worn or put away in the morning. For clothes that hang up on clothes-hangers: All hangers go in the same direction, with the hanger's hook facing away from you; shirts, blouses and jackets hang with the buttons (the front of the garment) facing the same direction.

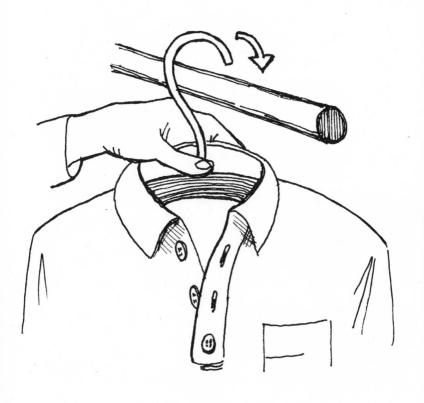

Figure 2.8.

2.9. Alarm clock

If one party can hear another party's alarm clock (in the same room or through a thin wall) and the parties are not getting up at the same time, the alarm should go off for no longer than five seconds; the snooze button hit no more than three times.[10]

2.10. Pets in bedrooms

For parties who share a bedroom (but not the pets), the House Rule is that pets are not allowed to enter the bedroom if one party objects.

2.11. Shoes on the bed

No shoes on the bed. This includes getting on the bed and keeping one's shod feet hanging over the edge.

2.12. Shoeless bedrooms

Whether to have a shoeless house is a separate issue and is addressed in §5.15. If the parties have agreed that wearing shoes in the house

---

[10] We recognize that it is almost impossible for some people to control their inability to wake up. We hope, however, that they will make an effort and that the other party will be patient.

is acceptable, this does not preclude the issue of shoes in a shared bedroom being addressed separately. The rule is that if shoes are allowed in the house, they are allowed in a shared bedroom. If the parties have their own bedrooms, the rule is that any party can declare his or her bedroom to be shoeless.

2.13. Towels from the bathroom

Some parties prefer to wrap themselves in their bath towel and wear it into the bedroom rather than using a robe. This is allowed, but the towel must be returned to the bathroom soon thereafter. Do not place damp towels on the bed or drape them over items that could be damaged. (Almost any furniture, including some plastic furniture, is likely to be damaged by prolonged contact with a damp towel.)

2.14. Trash

Only paper waste should be kept in a bedroom wastebasket. Food and other items must be disposed of in the kitchen or bathroom. Used tissues must be discarded in the wastebasket, not on the floor or on a bedside table. Being in bed

is not an excuse. The simple solution is to keep a
wastebasket by the bed.

2.15. The top of the dresser

The top of the dresser is not to be used as
a storage area, even if the surface area is
apportioned off to individual parties. The strictly
limited exception is overnight storage only; for
example, a watch, wallet, eyeglasses, jewelry
that's going to be put back on in the morning, or
loose change that's going back in one's pocket in
the morning.

Figure 2.15.

§3

The Laundry

3.1. Clean laundry

If one party prefers that folded towels and sheets be stacked on the shelves in a particular way (so that the fold is facing out, for example), that party's preference prevails—but only if that party folds the laundry at least as often as the party who is content with stacking the towels and sheets any which way.

All parties get to fold their own clothes as desired and cannot impose that style on another party. For example, if Jane does the laundry but doesn't want to fold Joe's underwear into neat little stacks, Jane is not required to. Of course, Joe is free to do it himself.

As stated in §2.8, for clothes that hang up on clothes-hangers: All hangers go in the same direction, with the hanger's hook facing away from you; shirts, blouses and jackets hang with the buttons (the front of the garment) facing the same direction.

3.2. Dirty laundry

Dirty clothes go into a hamper or other designated holding area. A corner of the bedroom floor is not an appropriate designated holding area.

Separate hampers for different kinds of clothes are not required. Clothes can be sorted at laundry time.

It should go without saying (one would hope) that basic laundry procedures must be followed: whites with whites, colors with colors, cold or lukewarm water for cotton clothing, etc. But these are not House Rules. The House Rule is simply that basic laundry practices must be followed. If one party has special rules for certain kinds of clothing, these should be worked out in advance. For example, if one party has a silk shirt that can't go into the dryer, this fact should be made known to all parties who do general laundry and the request must be followed. However, if you have a large number of special laundry instructions, you should consider a separate area (hamper, etc.) for these items so you can either wash them yourself or specify the instructions for the other party at laundry time.

Unless a member of the household works in a chicken-processing plant, biochemical lab or the like, it is acceptable to put clean clothes in a laundry basket that recently held dirty clothes.

3.3. Doing another party's laundry

Never do another's laundry without prior authorization. It is indeed with kind and thoughtful intentions that one would do another person's laundry, but it can backfire. And few things are as sharp as anger where one was expecting gratitude. There are two main reasons it can backfire. One is that some feel it to be an invasion of privacy. The other is the possibility of doing it wrong. Even if one is experienced at laundry and reads the "care" label, some people are idiosyncratic about how an article of clothing should be washed and dried.

3.4. Laundry left where others can see it
Refrain from hanging unsightly laundry, underwear, etc. to dry where guests or family members will come across it or where it will get

in the way, e.g., on the shower-curtain rod. A possible solution is to keep a small drying rack in the bedroom.

3.5. Laundry left in machines

Do not leave a load of laundry in the washer or dryer without providing a laundry basket or other handy receptacle for your housemate to throw your laundry in. If no receptacle is provided, clothes may be placed on top of the dryer (assuming the machine's design allows it). If there is no receptacle and the top of the dryer is not available, another party's wet clothes from the washing machine may be placed in the dryer—but do not start the dryer, as you do not know if all the clothes are supposed to be machine-dried. It is not acceptable to put wet laundry on top of beds, wooden chairs, or any other items that could be damaged.

If you live in a building in which you share laundry facilities with people you don't live with and you need to remove finished laundry from a machine, leave a polite note with the removed laundry suggesting that a receptacle be provided so that others are not forced to move laundry to a less-than-appropriate place. Word the note so that the other tenants believe you are genuinely concerned about preventing their clean laundry from getting dirty.[11]

3.6. Laundry detergent

The "last useful amount" rule (see §1.20) applies to laundry detergent, bleach, etc. the same as it does to food and other items. But more effort is often required to follow this rule for laundry because the shopping list is likely to be far from the laundry facilities. However, the extra effort required does not negate the rule.

---

[11] We suggest the following wording: "Hi, I had to move your laundry to use the machine. I hated to pile it on top of another machine [or on a chair, etc.] but had nowhere else. If in the future you leave a laundry basket nearby, I'd happily place your finished laundry in it."

§4

The Bathroom

4.1. The door

The House Rule: Leave the bathroom door partially open when not in use; a fully closed door indicates that the bathroom is occupied. If the door is closed, knock and wait for a response. If there is no response, you may enter.

It is important to note that this is the American bathroom-door rule. The custom in most other parts of the world is to keep the bathroom door closed at all times and to lock it when in use. Under this near-universal rule, someone wishing to use the bathroom can, but need not, knock first. If there is no response, you may try the door. However, you should not be surprised to find it locked despite no response, as the person using the bathroom may not feel like speaking. If any household members or frequent guests were not raised with the American bathroom-door rule, a hybrid rule is suggested: Leave the door open or closed when not in use, but *lock it when you use it*. Those not raised with the American bathroom-door rule will open a closed bathroom door without knocking as readily as they would open the door to a restroom in a restaurant.

4.2. Time spent in the bathroom

Too many variables exist to form a clear rule— number of people, number of bathrooms, and whether parties need to get ready in the morning at the same time. The general guideline is to be considerate and to apply common sense (a morning when everyone is getting ready for work is not the time to read on the toilet, for example). If scheduling problems arise, the parties should work out their own rule. Some simple math should work. In a three-person household, for example, if everyone gets up a half hour before leaving for work, each person gets ten minutes. The temptation to factor in gender should be avoided: e.g., men deserve more time because they have to shave; women deserve more time because they have to put on makeup.

Time spent in the shower should be factored into time spent in the bathroom. Shower time requires its own rule if long showers use up all the hot water or hot water is expensive.

4.3. The toilet seat and lid

Men must put the toilet seat up before urinating and must put it down when done. This is a hard and fast rule, not open for discussion[12] and not subject to compromise or tradeoffs. Whether to

---

[12] Well, we suppose it deserves at least a footnote of discussion. We are well aware of the argument: "Girls, get real. The seat goes back down as easily as it goes up." This is true. It's also true that bureau drawers close as easily as they open, as do cabinet doors, etc., but no one seems to be advancing this fact in favor of leaving drawers left pulled out and doors left open. One reason advanced for putting the seat back down is that if a woman gets up in the middle of the night to use the toilet, in the dark or blinded by the light suddenly turned on, it is very unpleasant to sit accidentally on the porcelain rim (or fall all the way into the toilet). If there is a woman in the household, this reason alone is enough. But even when there is not, the seat goes back down. This hides a fact that most men turn a blind eye to: the toilet rim gets drips and splatters that are best hidden, and putting the seat down does an adequate job between regular cleanings.

put the lid down is optional and may depend on such things as keeping the dog from drinking out of the toilet (or, of course, allowing the dog to drink out of the toilet).

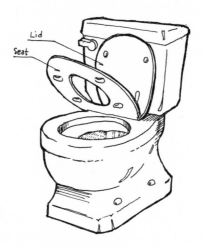

4.4. The toilet environs

Nothing should be stored on the floor within 18 inches of the toilet bowl except a toilet brush and a wastebasket. This means that such common items as a magazine rack, if on the floor, must be at least 18 inches from the toilet bowl. An exception to the rule is if no men ever use that toilet, even as guests. There is a very good rationale for the rule, but we would rather not discuss it.

4.5. The toilet paper

The House Rule is that the toilet paper should hang over and out, away from the wall. But if a female household member has a strong preference for the toilet paper to hang over and in, against the wall, that preference prevails. It is admittedly an odd preference[13], but women use toilet paper far more often than men—hence the rule.

A spare roll should always be within reach, with the top of the tank the preferred spot. Whoever uses the last of a roll (or the last useful amount of the roll) has to replace it. This rule stands despite the previously stated fact that women use more toilet paper than men.[14] If you use the last of the toilet paper and there is no more, the universal signal for this is to close the toilet lid and place the empty roll on top of it. Immediate steps should then be taken to procure more toilet paper.

---

[13] Some people prefer the paper against the wall to prevent unrolling by their cat. This is a reasonable argument, but it's better to train the cat.

[14] There is a myth about men replacing the toilet paper that is well expressed by the joke: "How many men does it take to replace a roll of toilet paper?" Answer: "Nobody knows, it's never been done." This myth is based on the fact that women use toilet paper approximately five times more often than men, and the more frequently a person uses the toilet paper, the more likely it is that that person will be using it when it runs out.

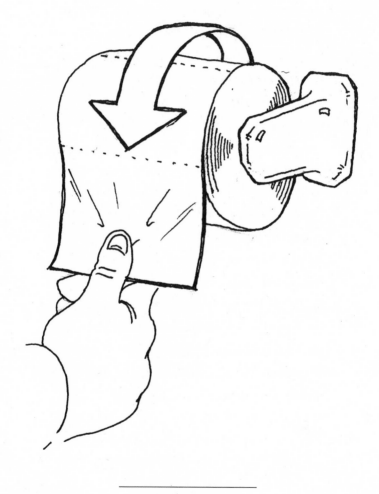

Figure 4.5.

4.6. Flushing the toilet

The general rule is to flush the toilet after each use, but this is a good area in which to agree on exceptions. Where water is expensive or in short supply, where sewerage treatment is an issue, for environmental concerns, or if it's late at night and the noise would disturb people, there is no harm in refraining from flushing the toilet after it's been used only for urinating. Do not flush the toilet while someone is taking a shower unless your plumbing system is such that doing so would have no effect on the water temperature in the shower.

4.7. Pets drinking out of the toilet

If all parties fully agree that it is acceptable for pets to drink out of the toilet, it is. Otherwise, no. People who find this behavior acceptable typically fall into one of two categories: those who think it's fine because dogs and cats are so cute that they can do no wrong; those who find dogs and cats rather gross, and drinking out of the toilet is just one of their many gross behaviors.

4.8. Cleaning the toilet after a single use

The toilet brush next to the toilet is not there just for scheduled cleaning. If a person has used the toilet and left it visibly soiled, the House Rule is that that person should immediately use the toilet brush (or toilet paper) to remedy the situation. We would prefer not to explain "visibly soiled."

4.9. The toilet tank as storage area

The back of the toilet (i.e., the top of the toilet tank) should be used only to store a roll of toilet paper. No box of tissues. No magazines. For the rationale, see House Rule 4.4, "The toilet environs."

Figure 4.9.

4.10. Female "sanitary products"

A box of tampons can be kept on the back of the toilet if, and only if, the parties have adopted an exception to the rule regarding placing things on the back of the toilet. If the sight of such products makes one of the parties uncomfortable, you might ask that party why the sight of toilet paper doesn't cause similar discomfort.

4.11. The wastebasket

The House Rule: Unsightliness is to be avoided. Used cotton swabs, pieces of toilet paper that have dabbed up shaving cuts, hair from the drain and the like should be stuffed down into the trash out of immediate sight or wrapped in a piece of tissue or toilet paper. Bathroom wastebaskets should have plastic liners.

4.12. Teeth brushing and flossing

The cap goes back on the toothpaste tube after each use. If a flip clap, it flips back closed. When placing the cap on the counter, place the cap up so that it doesn't leave little toothpaste rings. The buildup of encrusted toothpaste around the cap should be cleaned off occasionally. If the tube is the kind that can be rolled up from the bottom, it should be, but most brands come in a plastic tube and it does little good to squeeze from the bottom.

As noted in the Preamble, some habits are hard to break, and there is almost always an easier solution. For conflicts over toothpaste, simply purchase two (or more) tubes. Assigning an individual toothpaste tube to a party having difficulty following the House Rules costs no more money in the long run and takes up very little space. Those who care about the cap and how the tube should be squeezed can use the regular tube; those for whom it is a matter of indifference can use (and may only use) their own tube. If the non-capped tube causes a mess, however— toothpaste oozing out onto the counter, for example—steps must be taken to prevent this, perhaps by keeping the tube in a cup.

Do not leave the water running while brushing. There are three reasons for this rule: (1) there is no need for it; (2) it wastes water, and there is no reason to waste water even in areas where water is plentiful; and (3) even though it probably shouldn't, it drives most people crazy.

Flossing in front of the bathroom mirror inevitably leaves little flecks on the mirror. These should be cleaned off immediately because (1) they harden otherwise, and (2) that way you'll only be cleaning your own specks. The bathroom is the only proper place for flossing[15].

4.13. The soap in the shower

As a general rule, leaving hairs on the soap is not allowed. There is a simple solution, however, for those hairy people who (understandably) don't want to stand in the shower, cold and wet, picking their hairs off the soap: Use a separate bar of soap. It will be necessary to get different brands or colors to identify ownership. And one of those showerhead racks may be necessary— even houses with two-car garages seem to have only one built-in soap dish per shower unit.

If you use the last useful amount of a shared item such as a bar of soap or a bottle of shampoo,

[15] Or perhaps on the back porch, in the dark.

Figure 4.13.

replace the item. If a bar of soap is down to a sliver, replace it. Unfortunately, the mind seems to wander during early morning showers, and by the time one has left the shower, the sliver of soap has been forgotten. This should not be seen as an indication of lack of consideration; it's just the nature of early morning showers. When you notice the soap is down to a sliver or the shampoo bottle is almost empty, place it on the edge of the tub rather than back in its usual area. Even if you forget about the replacement as you towel yourself off, the next person to use the shower will notice the item on the edge of the tub and get a replacement.

4.14. Wiping down the shower/bathtub

It is not necessary to wipe down the tub or shower walls after each use. In the morning before work, there simply isn't time. Nor is it a desirable activity after a relaxing evening bath. Regular cleaning with modern-day products should easily take care of any soap scum or bathtub rings.

4.15. The tub and shower in general

Remove hair from the drain after each bath or

shower. This is a very hard rule to learn if one wasn't raised with it. Thus, if the next person to use the shower has to remove the hair, it is acceptable for that person to leave the glob of hair on the edge of the tub. This action should not be construed as mean or petty, but as a thoughtful reminder of the existence of the rule and the other party's failure to remember it.

If you have a tub/shower combination and the plumbing is such that the shower has to be manually changed from shower to tub, change it back to the tub setting when done; i.e., don't leave it so that when the next person leans into the tub and turns on the water, he or she gets sprayed on the back of the neck with cold water.

§4: The Bathroom

The shower curtain should be spread out after use so it can dry. For the same reason, a shower door should be closed when the shower is not in use.

4.16. Using another party's toiletries

Decide in advance if household members will share everyday items such as shampoo and shaving cream; otherwise, don't assume you can help yourself to another party's toiletries.

4.17. Towels

Each party gets his or her own bath towel and face towel. Rather than create more laundry, this system prevents excess laundry because it's easier to keep track of when the towels need washing. If space is limited, the face towel is hung over one's bath towel. The use of two bath towels per person is allowed (some people like one for hair, the other for body), but again if space is limited, such people are nevertheless limited to hanging space for one bath towel.

Do not use someone else's towel.

Bath towels may be dropped on the floor after use only if both of two conditions are met: (1) you have a house cleaner, and (2) you don't like your house cleaner. Otherwise, towels get hung up, spread out as much as possible, on the towel rack. If there isn't enough towel-rack space, towels can be draped over the shower-curtain rod. Each party is entitled to an equal amount of towel-hanging space. Thus, two-bath-towel people may feel a space shortage. A drying rack in one's bedroom is a possible solution.

Assuming one shower/bath per day, the norm is a fresh towel per week. Thus, that is also the House Rule.

A hand towel should always be next to the sink. It should be very clean. What might be clean enough for a couple to share might not be clean enough for a guest.

4.18. The bathroom sink and cabinet

Alas, in the average bathroom there is a woeful lack of space in the sink/vanity area. Ideally, the sink and counter would always be clear of clutter and everything one needs readily available in the bathroom cabinet. Also in this ideal world, when we engage in our various activities before the sink, we would be wide-awake and tolerant. Instead, it's a crowded little area, frequently used when we are pressed for time and not fully awake. It is difficult to have hard and fast rules under these circumstances, and patience is essential. Nevertheless, here are the House Rules:

Nothing other than soap, and perhaps a sponge, should be left within the immediate area of the sink, i.e., on the sink rim or within an inch of it. Each person using the sink should keep his or her own frequently used items in a designated area. For example, a man might place a face cloth on the vanity counter and keep on it his razor, shaving cream, hair brush, personal toothpaste tube, and toothbrush (unless he keeps this in a built-in toothbrush holder). A woman might have a similar area for her items. A small basket is useful for keeping items such as makeup and hair products orderly. A third area can be designated for shared items, if any, such as dental floss and contact lens solution. It may be easier to say what the rule isn't. It is *not* the rule that the bathroom vanity be kept totally clear, with everything put away in the cabinet after each use. It is also *not* the rule that whatever you use in front of the vanity can be left on the vanity counter.

The sink and immediate area must be given a quick clean after each use. A sponge kept on the edge of the sink[16] is an efficient method. It can be used to wipe up water splashed on the counter and to wash away shaving stubble and escaped globs of toothpaste from the sink.

---

[16] Note that this is the bathroom sink sponge and is *not* to be used in any other area of the bathroom.

§5

The Rest of the House

The rules in this section are in fact general House Rules that apply most often to "the living room," with the living room broadly defined to mean whatever room or rooms serve as a common area where household members spend leisure time. Thus, reference to "living room" can be read as applying to any other room, as appropriate. For example, if you have a very large kitchen with a corner set aside as a reading area, living room rules would apply.

5.1. Neatness level in general

It is difficult to articulate a clear rule on neatness while maintaining the general principle that the living room is for living. The following coffee table rule can serve as a guideline for other issues: If the coffee table has magazines stored on it, a magazine you've picked up goes back on the coffee table. But only "back on" the table. It is not necessary to put it back in a dressed-and-covered arrangement such as you might find in a doctor's waiting room when you're the first patient of the day. On the other hand, if one is interrupted in the middle of an article, the magazine may be left open, provided that you return to it soon thereafter. It is not dropped on the floor or the couch. It is returned to the coffee table. Indeed, nothing is left on the couch.

If eating is allowed in the living room (which is covered by House Rule 5.3), dishes, glasses, soda cans, etc. are removed immediately—even more immediately than they would be removed from the dining room or kitchen table.

5.2. The coffee table

Part of the coffee table rule was previously set forth. Here is the rest of the rule: Do not use magazines for drink coasters. The coffee table is not a catch basin for household jetsam such as loose change, spare pens and pencils, mail, a purse, sunglasses, etc. Feet never go on the coffee table.

5.3. Eating in the living room

The coffee table may be used for coffee and snacks. Regular meals must be eaten at the dining room or kitchen table.

5.4. Things you can't do in the living room

Don't do in the living room anything you would normally do in the bathroom or bedroom. This means you cannot clip or file your nails in the living room. It also means you can't nap in the living room. Although the person who wants to nap on the couch may claim that he or she doesn't require others to move around quietly, refrain from playing music, or make any other accommodations, it is quite difficult for the non-napping people to go about business as usual. As this rationale indicates, an exception to the no-napping rule is if there is no one else home, or if everyone is going to nap at the same time. Unlike such behavior as clipping one's nails in the living room[17], there is nothing inherently wrong with sleeping in the living room.

---

[17] The issue with clipping one's nails is not just that it is inappropriate public grooming, but that some clippings, no matter how much care is taken, will land where someone else will come across them.

5.5. Storing mail

Incoming mail should have a designated holding area. This should be in a common area and easily in sight. Unfortunately, this area will often have to be in the living room (if in a basement den, for example, the mail will be forgotten and bills left unpaid; if in the kitchen, the mail will be subject to food stains). The mail area should be kept small and self-contained. Mail can be placed in a decorative basket, for example, or in a shoebox.

If one or more parties have a habit of not taking their mail from the holding area, so that it tends to overflow, establish a second holding area for old mail. Any party may then remove old mail (mail that's been around several days) from the holding area for current mail to the holding area for old mail. When the old-mail holding area gets full, it must be emptied. There is a lot of room here for developing personalized rules. For instance, a household might have one area for bills and official-looking letters, another area for junk mail and magazines—but avoid turning the living area into an office.

Figure 5.5.

5.6. The phone

Do not use the living room for extended phone calls unless there is no other option; e.g., there is no portable handset or other room to which one could reasonably retire. Otherwise, take your cell phone or mobile handset into another room, such as the bedroom.

There is no excuse for not taking messages for other household members. This includes writing down that there is a new message for another party if you are the first to access the answering machine or voice mail.

5.7. Music

If one party wants to listen to music and the other doesn't, there is no firm rule. If only occasional conflicts of interest arise, the general rule is that the desires of the person who wants to listen to music prevail because it's easier for the non-listening person to go to another room than it is to move the stereo system. Keep headphones in mind (but no singing along, dancing, or wild gesturing). If the non-listening person is reading, perhaps music without lyrics will not be a disruption.

CDs: When playing CDs, place the empty cases on top of the player or put them consistently in a similarly designated area. And when taking CDs out of the CD player, put them back in their cases. This is a very difficult rule for many to follow. Nevertheless, it is a hard and fast rule:

There should never be even a single loose CD lying around. The cased CD should also go back into the CD rack, but this rule is more flexible. It is acceptable to allow several CD cases to pile up before putting them away in the rack.

5.8. Television

The remote: There is no House Rule on the use of the remote for channel surfing. It is beyond civilized control. But there are rules on the use of the television.

The TV should not be on during dinner (supper). If one or more parties wish to watch a program during the time reserved for dinner (the evening news, for example), dinnertime should be adjusted to accommodate this desire. But if it is not practical to adjust dinnertime, the rule stands: No television during dinner.

If you have company, the TV should be off (unless, of course, the company has come over specifically to watch a particular program).

The TV should not be used for background ambiance. If the TV is on, it should be watched and conversation limited so as not to interfere with the program.

5.9. Reading the newspaper

When done with a section, do not leave it open.

Refold each section to its original order.

Reading interesting items aloud to another person who is also reading the paper should be very limited. It's nice to share one's interests and especially nice for friends or couples to make reading the paper an activity they can enjoy together. On the other hand, it can be very frustrating to read a sentence, get interrupted, go back to the paper, find your place, read the sentence again, get interrupted, etc. until you realize you've read the same sentence five times.

5.10. Leaving lights on

There is no official House Rule on turning off lights, only some information.

Contrary to popular belief, it is not true that turning a light on and off frequently causes surges of electricity and thus costs more than leaving the light on. If it drives you crazy to see a light left on unnecessarily, you may have internalized some rules from an earlier time when electricity and light bulbs were much more expensive. Today, burning a 75-watt bulb costs a fraction of a cent per hour[18]. On the other hand, most households use more than one bulb and leave them on for more than an hour. Those fractions add up. There are millions of people in America. The energy use adds up.

5.11. Windows and shades

Windows should be closed when the heat or air conditioning is on. Shades should be pulled down (or blinds closed) in the evening and up during the day, unless closed to block summer sun.

5.12. Décor

The same rule on décor for the bedroom applies to the rest of the house or apartment. We repeat it here, with an additional comment. The issue with décor is when one party wants a particularly distinctive style—pink and frilly, for example, or guns and mounted moose heads on the walls. The House Rule: No extremes.

Another décor rule is that no one owns extra rights to décor selection. The following are just a few of the many reasons that do *not* give one

---

[18] Based on a national average of eight cents per kilowatt hour.

person extra say in décor: being a woman; being gay; having an art degree; having been raised in a rich family; or making a greater financial contribution to the household.

5.13. Cleaning other people's knickknacks, antiques, etc.

This rule has the same rationale as the rule on doing other people's laundry: You may do more harm than good. What to you looks like tarnish could be 100-year-old patina to the owner. Don't clean or even dust another party's knickknacks, etc. without prior approval.

5.14. Clothes on furniture

Unlike the bedroom rule, which allows clothes to be draped on furniture under limited circumstances, the House Rule for the living room is stricter: No clothes on the furniture. Use the coat closet or the coat rack, if you have either. Otherwise, parties must bring their coats and other clothes into their bedrooms. If there is room and all parties agree, a chair may be placed near the front door to serve as a coat rack.

5.15. The shoeless house

In much of the world, people would no more wear shoes in their house than you would put your shod feet on the furniture. The shoeless house is becoming more common in America. But for now, the rule is that shoes are worn in the house unless the parties agree otherwise.[19]

5.16. Houseguests

True guests can do nothing wrong: proper etiquette requires that any wrongdoing be

---

[19] The authors highly recommend the shoeless house. It's more comfortable, feels more homey, and after a while you'll wonder how you could ever have brought that street dirt into the house. When visiting, look for a lineup of shoes just inside the door. (But you may not force the rule on your own houseguests.)

ignored.[20] Houseguests, on the other hand—those who stay a week or more—are another matter. It seems they can do nothing right. This rule does not address how houseguests should behave, but rather, how household members should treat each other when houseguests are present.

This is a two-part rule: (1) exercise patience and understanding toward your guests and (2) exercise patience and understanding toward the household member who is the primary host (e.g., your spouse would be the primary host for your in-laws; you would be the primary host for your old college friends).

The rationale for part (1) is that it is not as easy as one assumes to be a guest. It's a bit like being in a foreign country—guests don't know your customs and rules. They may not even own a copy of this book. If a guest takes a shower and drops the towel on the floor, it may be because the guest is an inconsiderate slob. On

---

[20] See generally, *Miss Manners' Guide to Domestic Tranquility*, Martin, J., New York, 1999. The book offers marvelous advice on houseguests and many other sensitive topics.

the other hand, the guest may assume that the universal House Rule for towels is that they are used only once and left on the floor (because in hampers they get moldy) until the person whose turn it is to do the laundry that week does a laundry. The rationale for part (2) is that the primary host is suffering the same strain from having houseguests that you are, but with three additional strains: being the primary host; concern about how the guests' behavior reflects on the primary host; and concern about how the guests are affecting the rest of the household members.

§6

The Exterior

6.1. The shared hallway

If you live in a building with a shared stairwell or hallway, put nothing in the area outside your door but a doormat. An especially egregious violation of this rule is setting the bagged-up trash outside one's door with the intention of taking it down to the trash bin at a more convenient time.

6.2. The porch

Any furniture on the porch should be designed for porches; for example, moving your old living room couch onto the porch is not allowed.

6.3. Smoking outdoors

For those who smoke, stepping outside for a cigarette has become an admirable practice, and we hesitate to impose rules on this already considerate behavior. Thus, there is only one House Rule: Get rid of the cigarette butt properly. For some reason, many smokers who would be appalled to see someone drop a candy wrapper on the ground think nothing of dropping a cigarette butt on the ground. If there is an outdoor ashtray, use it; if not, bring an ashtray with you. If this isn't practical, consider what soldiers on base call "field stripping" a cigarette: Pinch off the hot ash. Rip the paper and dump the tobacco in your hand, then scatter it in the grass. Roll the paper into a tiny ball

and either throw in the grass (if there is plenty of grass and not many other people are doing the same thing) or put it in your pocket. Put the filter in your pocket.

The rule on how far from the house the smoker must be: Only far enough so that the smoke does not drift back into the house. It all depends on whether doors or windows are open and which way the wind is blowing.

6.4. The shared automobile

The authors consider the shared automobile an extension of the household to a limited degree and address it accordingly. Driving styles and skills are not discussed.

6.5. Parking

If you have a garage, the automobile should be kept in the garage. It goes in forward (not backed-in). If the parties agree that the automobile can be left in the driveway (often the case in areas of the country where people tend to use their garage for storage), then the automobile also goes into the driveway forward, not backed-in. This don't-back-in rule does not apply if road conditions dictate otherwise—a busy street that would be dangerous to back into, for example, or an imminent snowstorm. Another exception is if backing into the road is illegal.

6.6. Shutting down the automobile

Once the automobile is parked, the music system is shut off. The air conditioning is shut off. The heater/defroster fan is shut off. The rearview mirrors are left as the last driver used them, even if the next person will have to readjust them. The seat is likewise left as the last driver used it. An exception to the seat rule is if the heights of the people driving the automobile vary so much that the tall person can't get into the automobile without first reaching in and sliding the seat back. If such is the case, the short person should slide the seat back before getting out. The tall person is not required to slide the seat forward after use (because with the seat back, the short person can still get into the automobile).

6.7. The handbrake

The handbrake (often called the parking brake
and occasionally called the emergency brake) is
put on when parked, even with automobiles that
have automatic transmissions. The rationale:
(1) if the handbrake is on and the automobile is
bumped hard by another vehicle (as sometimes
happens when parked on the street), having
the handbrake on will provide some protection
against damage to the transmission; (2) if a
manual transmission, putting the automobile in
gear is not enough of a brake on an incline; (3)
if the automobile is accidentally knocked out of

gear, the handbrake will prevent it from rolling away (particularly important if there might be children left in the automobile); and (4) if not used regularly, the handbrake might rust up and not be available when needed.

This rule, however, is open to amendment. The rationale for those in favor of not using the handbrake: (1) if the handbrake is on in the winter, the handbrake can freeze up and get stuck; (2) putting the automobile in "park" provides enough protection except on the steepest of inclines, and in those rare situations the handbrake can be deployed and the wheels turned to the curb; (3) putting an automobile in park and setting the handbrake is like wearing a belt while wearing suspenders.

6.8. Maintaining the automobile interior

Travel litter: Coffee cups, food wrappers, etc. must be removed or placed in a container. The container must be emptied when full (see §1.27, "Taking out the trash"). The House Rule on air fresheners: No air fresheners. The glove compartment (also known by more contemporary names, such as map box, but none seem to stick) and the trunk should not be used as mobile storage containers. Keep in them only what is directly related to convenience and safety in the use of the vehicle.

6.9. Gasoline

The "last useful amount" rule applies as set forth in §1.20. The parties should agree in advance on what the minimum amount is that can be left in the tank. In an area with easy access to 24-hour gas stations, for example, the parties might agree to a quarter of a tank. Or they might decide there should be enough to get to work and back. Do not leave the vehicle with less than the agreed-upon amount.

Acknowledgement

Co-author David E. O'Connor feels unable to claim full credit for the House Rules contained herein. He did not so much invent them as compile and edit them. They came from a lifetime of observation and, mainly, from contributed suggestions of dozens of people who have their own rule on a particular issue or a desire for a rule to exist. Thus, the co-author E.L. Henderson, who is everyone who ever said: This is how it should be done.

—E.L. Henderson

About Co-Author David E. O'Connor

David O'Connor grew up in a family of seven in a three-bedroom, one-bath home (his first introduction to the challenges of shared living space). While serving in the United States Army as a young man, he lived with fellow soldiers for six months in barracks and for two-and-a-half years in an isolated seven-person station—which was, aside from its military function, essentially a two-bedroom, one-bath home surrounded by barbed wire.

David has shared apartments and houses with various roommates; with his first wife; his wife and their child; a second wife; the second wife and the child from the first marriage; and, of course, he has lived alone.

After earning a bachelor's degree in English and a master's degree in special education, he later went on to receive his doctorate in law. David is also a certified mediator. As an attorney he has represented landlords, tenants, accused murderers, wives, and husbands. He has published works on education, labor law, legislation, and criminal law, and he has also edited law journals and documents for state government and the United Nations. David is currently a freelance writer and editor in Bozeman, Montana.

Index

A

Alarm clock, 2.9
Appliances, small, on countertop, 1.12
Automobile, in general, 6.4-6.9

B

Bathroom
    door, 4.1
    in general, 4.1-4.18
    sink and cabinet, in general, 4.18
    time spent in, 4.2
    when occupied, 4.1
Bed
    making, 2.3
    shoes on, 2.11
    things allowed in, 2.5
    which side to sleep on, 2.1
Bedroom
    bath towels in, 2.13
    décor, 2.4
    dresser, *see* Dresser
    in general, 2.1-2.15
    pets in, 2.10
    pillows on floor, 2.2
    shoeless, in general, 2.12
    temperature, 2.7
    trash in, 2.14
Blender blades, in dishwasher, 1.1
Bliss, domestic, PREAMBLE
Bread, resealing, 1.19
Bric-a-brac, *see* Knickknacks
Brillo pads, 1.24, 1.25
Brushing teeth, number of times,
    PREAMBLE
Bureau, *see* Dresser

C

Cans, alignment of, *see* Compulsive
Cats, *see* Pets
Causation, correlation vs., 1.8
CDs, putting away, 5.7

Chef, *see* Cooking
China, *see* Glasses
Cigarettes, *see* Smoking
Cleaning
    after cooking, when, 1.23
    by dinner guests, 1.24
    cooking vs., 1.22
    rules for kitchen, in general, 1.25
Clock, alarm, 2.9
Clothes
    in bedroom, 2.8
    on furniture, 5.14
    washing, *see* Laundry
Coffee dregs, in dishwasher, 1.1
Coffee grounds, in sink, 1.8
Coffee table
    eating from, 5.3
    in general, 5.2, 5.1
Compact Discs, *see* CDs
Compromise, PREAMBLE
Compulsive alignment of food on
    shelves, 1.13
Cook, one-at-a-time rule, 1.21
Cooking
    in general, 1.21
    vs. cleaning, 1.22
Correlation, causation vs., 1.8
Countertops, preparing food on, 1.10
Crystal, *see* Glasses
Cutting boards
    when required, 1.11
    wood vs. plastic, 1.11

D

Décor
    bedroom, 2.4
    no special rights to choice of, 5.12
    rest of the house, 5.12
Dinner guests
    cleaning up by, 1.24
    vs. house guests, 1.2

Dishes,
    loading in dishwasher, 1.1
    pet, washing, 1.5
    soaking in sink, 1.3
    washing all at once, 1.3
    washing by hand, 1.4
    washing item-by-item, 1.3
    when dishwasher is full, 1.3
Dishwasher,
    loading, in general, 1.1
    two, use of, 1.2
    unloading, in general, 1.2
Dogs, *see* Pets
Dresser, things on top of, 2.15
Drinking from container, 1.16

E
Eating
    from container, 1.16
    in living room, 5.3
    sink, 1.14
    standing up, 1.14
    without plate, 1.14
Electric lights, *see* Lights
Exterior, in general, 6.1-6.9

F
Feet, men, bigger, 2.2
Flatware, *see* Silverware
Flossing teeth
    in bathroom, 4.12
    in bed, *see* Bedroom
Food
    on shelves, 1.13
    preparing, on counters, 1.10
Forks, *see* Silverware

G
Garage, *see* Automobile
Gasoline, *see* Automobile
Gender, generalization about, 2.1
Glasses, on shelf, 1.6, PREAMBLE
Globalization, delayed, 1.3

Grandparents, humoring, 1.12

H
Hair
    in drain, 4.13
    on soap, 4.13
Hallway, shared, 6.1
Houseguests
    dinner guests vs., 1.24
    in general, 5.16
Hoyle, on cards, PREAMBLE

I
Ice cream, from container, *see* Eating
Icebox, *see* Refrigerator

J
Juice container, *see* Milk and juice
    container

K
Kitchen, in general, 1.1-1.27
Knickknacks, cleaning of other people's,
    5.13
Knives, *see* Silverware

L
Last of something, *see* Last useful amount
    rule
Last Useful Amount Rule, defined, 1.20
Laundry
    clean, folding, 3.1
    clean, hanging in public, 3.4
    detergent, last of, 3.6
    dirty, 3.2
    doing other people's, 3.3
    in general, 3.1-3.6
    left in machine, 3.5
Le Cordon Bleu, 1.21
Lights, electric, leaving on, 5.10
Living room,
    forbidden activities in, 5.4
    in general, 5.1-5.16

Luncheon meat, boiled, 1.21

M
Mail, storing, 5.5
Martin, J., *see* Miss Manners
Milk
    and juice containers, leaving open,
    1.18
    from container, *see* Drinking
Mirror, bathroom, cleaning, 4.12
Miss Manners, 5.16
Music
    listening to, 5.7
    see also, CDs

N
Nails
    clipping in bed, 2.5
    clipping in living room, 5.4
Napping in living room, 5.4
Neatness, in general, 5.1
Newspaper
    reading aloud, 5.9
    refolding after use, 5.9, PREAMBLE

P
Pet dishes, washing, 1.5
Pets
    drinking out of toilet, 4.7
    in bedroom, 2.10
Petty issues, fighting over, PREAMBLE
Phone
    messages, taking, 5.6
    use of, 5.6
Pillows and bolsters on floor, 2.2
Pillows, decorative, 2.3
Plumber, hourly rate of, 1.8
Porch, 6.2

R
Recycling, *see* Trash and recyclables
Refrigerator, leaving door open, 1.17
Refueling in flight, *see* Eating

Rest of the House, 5.1-5.16
Robert's Rules of Order, PREAMBLE

S
Sanitary products, in bathroom, 4.10
Sex, lack of rule on, 2.6
Shades, *see* Windows and shades
Shampoo, last of, 4.13
Sheets, how to put on bed, 2.2
Shelves
    food stored on, 1.13
    kitchen, glasses on, 1.6
Shoeless house, 5.15
Shoes, *see* Shoeless house
Shower
    soap in, 4.13
    time spent in, 4.2
    using, in general, 4.15
    wiping down after use, 4.14
Silverware
    in dishwasher, 1.1
    in drawer, 1.7
Simpsons, The, 1.27
Sink
    cleaning with bleach, steel wool, 1.25
    eating, *see* Eating
Smoking, 6.3
Soap,
    hairs on, 4.13
    last of, 4.13
SOS pads, 1.25
Sous chef, *see* Cooking
Spam luncheon meat, 1.21
Sponge
    bathroom, 4.18
    cellulous vs. sea, 1.9
    dry and useless vs. wet and moldering,
    1.9
    kitchen, use of, 1.9
Spoons, *see* Silverware

T
Tampons, *see* Sanitary products

Teeth brushing and flossing, 4.12
Telephone, *see* Phone
Television, watching, 5.8
Temperature, room, *see* Bedroom
Toaster
    on countertop, *see* Appliances, small
    unplugged, 1.12
Toenail clippings, *see* Nails
Toilet
    cleaning after one use, 4.8
    environs, 4.4
    flushing, when, 4.6
    paper, indicating last of, 4.5
    paper, replacing, 4.5, PREAMBLE
    pets drinking out of, 4.7
    seat, 4.3, PREAMBLE
    tank, as storage area, 4.9
Toiletries, using another's, 4.16
Toothpaste cap, noncompliance with
    rule, PREAMBLE
Towels
    bath, in bedroom, 2.13
    in general, 4.17
Trash
    and recyclables, 1.26
    bathroom, 4.11
    bedroom, 2.14
    kitchen, taking out, 1.27
Tub, *see* Shower
TV, *see* Television

V
Vanity, *see* Bathroom sink

W
Washing dishes *see* Dishes
Water, boiling without cover, *see*
    Cooking
Windows and shades, 5.11
World Bank, late for work at, 1.3

An Invitation

The authors invite readers to continue to share with us their own house rules and petty grievances. We also welcome any questions or comments about the rules we have included— or neglected to include—in this edition. Use the following blank pages for notes and submit proposed topics at www.EastQuincyPublishing.com or write to:

Henderson's House Rules
c/o East Quincy Publishing
P.O. Box 851
Johnson City, TN 37605-0851

NEED A GREAT GIFT IDEA?

Henderson's House Rules is the perfect gift for housewarmings, graduations, engagements, weddings and anniversaries—or a fun "anytime" gift from one housemate to another.

Check your local bookstore, order online at www.EastQuincyPublishing.com, or use this form:

❧

Send me ___ copies of ***Henderson's House Rules*** for $12.95 each

Name: _____

Organization: _____

Address:_____

City, State, Zip:_____

Phone: _____

Email: _____

Please send a check or money order for $12.95 per book.
(Shipping and handling compliments of East Quincy Publishing)

❧

25. — J   Omaha → Lovela...
25. — L   540 mi
30. — J   ───────────
30. — L   (R PA?D TRAILER
70. — J   ───────────
60. — J   Loveland → Ogden 490
90. — J   (1030)
75. — L   Ogden → Boise — 310
(5.4+ — L)   (1340)
47. — L   ───────────
123. — J   Boise → B'ton
75. — L
40. — J   Hotel (Posie)
85. — L

J: 438.
L: 391.
─────────
T: 829. ÷ 2 = 415.

THINGS TO LOOK UP:
Portland cement
Farewell Bend, OR

Review Copy